# Butterflies

ABDO
Publishing Company

A Buddy Book
by
Julie Murray

## VISIT US AT
www.abdopub.com

Published by Buddy Books, an imprint of ABDO Publishing Company, 4940 Viking Drive, Suite 622, Edina, Minnesota 55435. Copyright © 2002 by Abdo Consulting Group, Inc. International copyrights reserved in all countries. No part of this book may be reproduced in any form without written permission from the publisher.

Printed in the United States.

Edited by: Christy DeVillier
Contributing Editors: Matt Ray, Michael P. Goecke
Graphic Design: Maria Hosley
Image Research: Deborah Coldiron
Cover Photograph: Eyewire Inc.
Interior Photographs: Corel, Minden Pictures

### Library of Congress Cataloging-in-Publication Data

Murray, Julie, 1969-
  Butterflies/Julie Murray.
      p. cm. — (Animal kingdom)
  Summary: An introduction to the physical characteristics, behavior, life cycle, and various habitats of butterflies.
  ISBN 1-57765-718-7
    1. Butterflies—Juvenile literature. [1. Butterflies.] I. Title. II. Animal kingdom (Edina, Minn.)

QL544.2 M87 2002
595.78'9—dc21

                                        2001055215

# Contents

# Insects

There are more than one million different species of insects. Butterflies, grasshoppers, ants, and bees are all insects. Insects live in the air, in water, and on land. You can find insects in icy lakes, steamy jungles, and hot deserts.

Butterflies are insects.

# Butterflies And Moths

There are more than 200,000 known species of butterflies and moths. Sometimes it is hard to tell the difference between a butterfly and a moth. Here are some helpful guidelines:

# Butterflies vs Moths

| | | |
|---|---|---|
| Most butterflies have bright colors. | ◄····► | Most moths have dull coloring. |
| Most butterflies fly in the daytime. | ◄····► | Moths mostly move around at night. |
| There are knobs on the end of a butterfly's antennae. | ◄····► | A moth's antennae are short, furry, and knob-free. |
| A butterfly rests with its wings folded upright. | ◄····► | A moth holds its wings flat when resting. |

# What They Look Like

Like all insects, a butterfly has six legs and a pair of antennae. Antennae are an insect's long feelers. Antennae help butterflies smell and keep balanced.

The three main body parts of butterflies and all insects are: the head, the thorax (middle), and the abdomen (stomach).

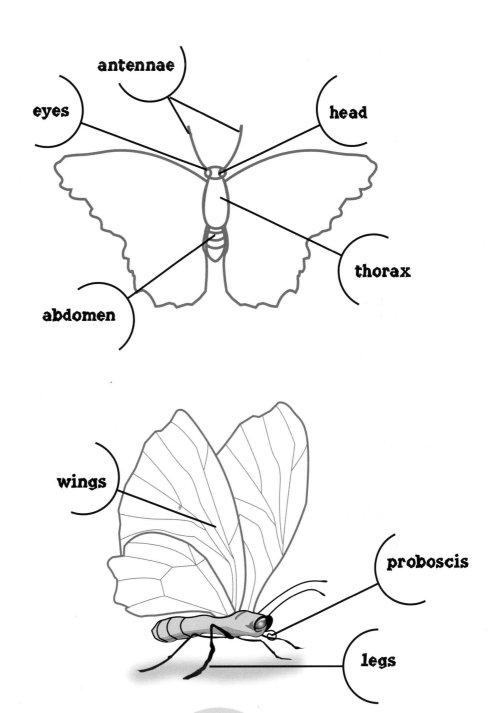

antennae

eyes

head

thorax

abdomen

wings

proboscis

legs

# Colors

Where do butterflies get their bright colors? Thousands of tiny scales are on a butterfly's wings. These scales give butterflies their colors and patterns. Each butterfly species has its own special colors and markings.

Like all butterflies, this variegated fritillary has tiny scales on its wings.

Some butterflies have tails on their wings, like this tiger swallowtail.

Some butterflies have marks that look like eyes.

Some butterflies rely on their colors to escape danger. Some animals will not eat butterflies of certain colors. These colors are a sign that a butterfly will taste bad. Also, some colors help butterflies hide from animals.

A butterfly's colors can be helpful for hiding.

# Eating

Butterflies eat using their proboscis. The proboscis is a long drinking tube. Butterflies use their proboscis like a straw to suck up food. Butterflies feed on flower nectar. Nectar is the sweet liquid plants make. Butterflies also eat tree sap and rotting fruit. A butterfly curls up its proboscis when it is not feeding.

Can you see this
butterfly's proboscis?

# Where They Live

Butterflies live everywhere except Antarctica. More than half of all butterfly species live in rain forests. These rain forests are warm and wet. So, many kinds of plants grow there. It is the perfect place for a butterfly!

Many butterflies live in rain forests.

Some butterflies migrate a long way each year. In the autumn, monarch butterflies migrate from Canada to Mexico. The monarch butterfly can fly 80 miles (128 km) in one day!

# Stages Of Life

Many female butterflies lay their sticky eggs on leaves. Some eggs hatch in a few days, but others take a few months. When the egg hatches, a caterpillar comes out.

Caterpillars hatch from butterfly eggs.

The newborn caterpillar begins eating right away. The growing caterpillar will molt when it grows too big for its skin. A molting caterpillar sheds its old skin. Growing caterpillars will molt many times.

When a caterpillar is full-grown, it stops eating. It sheds its skin for the last time. Then, the caterpillar grows a hard covering and turns into a chrysalis. This is the beginning of this insect's metamorphosis.

A caterpillar becomes a chrysalis.

Metamorphosis changed this chrysalis into a beautiful monarch butterfly.

During metamorphosis, the chrysalis changes. Metamorphosis can take two weeks, or a few months. When metamorphosis is complete, a winged insect breaks out of its chrysalis shell. The caterpillar has changed into a butterfly!

# Important Words

abdomen  the back part of an insect's body.

chrysalis  an insect that is changing from a caterpillar to a butterfly.

metamorphosis  changes that take place as a caterpillar becomes an adult butterfly.

migrate  to move from one place to another when the seasons change.

molt  to shed and grow new skin.

proboscis  the body part a butterfly uses for feeding.

species  living things that are very much alike.

thorax  the middle part of an insect's body.

# Web Sites

## Butterflies and Moths

www.butterflies-moths.com
Learn more about butterflies and moths at this picture-filled web site.

## Children's Butterfly Site

www.mesc.nbs.gov/butterfly/Butterfly.html
Designed for children, this web site features butterfly coloring pages, pictures, and more.

## A Third Grade Butterfly Web Project

www.acnatsci.org/education/l2l/butterflyhome.html
See caterpillars and butterflies up close and learn more about metamorphosis.

# Index